FRAGMENTS OF A D?

the autopsy of a love that dared to ruin me

VENUSIAN ALCHEMIST

A story written in the stars, bound by fire and shadow – this was how it all began.

The connection that felt like fate, as if the universe itself conspired to weave our paths together.

You, a force wrapped in mystery, with eyes that could pierce the soul,

And I, the woman who believed in the

Illusion of love's perfect symmetry.

What I didn't know, as you whispered

Promises in my ear, was that I was walking into a storm that would tear me apart and rebuild me.

Through the labyrinth of affection and betrayal, I learned to see you for what you were –

A dream woven from darkness, a mercenary mission I never signed up for, but one I emerged from alive, unscathed and free.

This is not just my story – it's the story of every woman who has been blinded by love's darkness, only to find the light within her own self again.

To you,

The architect of my undoing,

I write these words not for closure, but for remembrance.

You carved your name into my skin with poison laced with affection… and I wore it like a crown, blinded by the beauty of the scars.

But know this:

Even the darkest nights cannot hide the truth forever.

As I stand in the ashes of what we were, I dare to let the wind carry your memory away, piece by piece.

This is for me, for the woman that I became & survived…

and for you "Jupiter"

Who will never know peace again.

Chronicles of Emotion

The Attraction to Darkness
Fading Spark
Shadows in the Ether
Jupiter at 4am
Veil of Smoke
The Illusions I Was Sold
Naivete
The Space Between Us
Fingers in the Flame
The Ghosts We Were
A Rose with Thorns
Jupiter's Riddle
Jupiter's Game - Push & Pull
Under the Veil
My Wake
The Mirrors of Manipulation
Baia

Galileo Halo

Romantic Mercenary

The Silence That Was Left

Ricochet Effect

Emotional Sadism

Sanctuary

Limbo of What-Ifs

Discernment

You're Going to Text Me Soon

02:18am

Dismissed

Psychosis

Inner Conflict

Truths Carved in Lies

The Fading of a Misery

Something New

The Sting

Gulag

Plutonian Mermaid

Tangled in Your Own Web

Shattered

Dance at My Mercy

Ruin

How Far I've Fallen

I'll Hold My Breath Until You Do

When the Wound Was Self-Inflicted

Seeds of Doubt

Liberation

Venom

The Other Half of Me

Dust

From the Distance You Created

Seams

Tattoo

Last Face

That Sunday in September

Power Play

Consume You

Outrun

A Knight in Disguise

Unfixable & Void

Yemanjá

The Scar You Can't Hide

It's Almost Poetic

Self Destruction

In Retrospect

Mourning Moment in the Abyss

32nd

Walking in the Light of My Own Creation

How Insignificant You Have Become

Tainted

Kynthos

16:10

Not Really

Forged

The Void Left Behind

Thoughts in Thessaloniki

Acceptance

You Were the Lesson

Touche

Rapunzel Awakening

But in Spite of You

Farewell Jupiter

End Note

Epilogue of the Heart

About the Author

At first, your darkness was seductive,

a dance of shadows, promising warmth.

I fell in love with the power you exuded, the way you twisted me into knots and called it love.

but now I see it –

the allure was never yours, it was the emptiness inside me

that mistook your poison for passion

The Attraction to Darkness

In your arms, I believed I had
found home,
but I soon realized I was only a
visitor in your world,
waiting for the door to close.

Eu te amei, but I lost myself

Fading Spark

In the quiet, I hear your footsteps –
but you're not here.
Only the echo of promises,
and the weight of a love that never
reached the light.
I wore your lies like silk,
soft against my skin.
but now I burn with the truth

Shadows in the Ether

She was delicate, a rose with thorns,
her fragility a mirror to my strength.
I knew the power of her heart,
how I could break it and still have her
come back.

For her, I was the only choice.

For me, she was just another conquest.

Jupiter at 4am

I walked through the smoke of you – willingly, I followed the haze,

not knowing the fire was your reflection,

Now, the smoke is all that

remains… and you –

a wisp, a memory.

Veil of Smoke

You painted your words like a

masterpiece, each promise a

brushstroke of perfection.

But the canvas was cracked, the

colors bled into nothing.

I once believed in the lies you sold me,

but now, I see them for what they

are –

empty strokes,

leaving nothing behind

but the cold, barren space of a lie

The Illusions I Was Sold

Your kiss promised salvation,
but in its taste, I found only ashes,
each touch a deceit,
each word a trap,
and I walked willingly into it

Naivete

Once, the distance between us felt
unbearable,
but now, it's my sanctuary.

I used to long for your presence, to be
wrapped in your toxic arms, but now,
your absence is my solace.

I'm learning to love the quiet,
to fill the empty space with my own
breath

and I'll never look back

The Space Between Us

You touched my skin like fire,

it was the burn of your deceit,

slow… unbearable and sweet.

You whispered secrets but I tasted

the poison in your breath

I should have known that the

sweetest lies… were meant for

death

Fingers In The Flame

We danced in a dream of tangled lies,

whispers in the dark, beneath cloudy skies.

A touch that once felt like a promise kept

Now

lingers cold, where warmth once wept.

I wore my heart like a crown, so bright,

But it cracked in silence, in the depth of night.

You never saw the weight you left behind,

A soul betrayed,

a love confined.

The Ghosts We Were

I was your delicate rose,

untouched by the world

until you violently plucked me

from the earth

and crushed my petals beneath

the weight of your capricious

needs.

You only took.

A Rose with Thorns

I spoke in riddles, my love a puzzle
she could never quite piece together.
Each day she tried to decipher me,
but I was never meant to be
understood.
I was a riddle she would never solve
and that, in itself, was the power I
held over her.

Jupiter's Riddle

She never understood the game we played
the way I pulled her in just to push her away.
She thought it was love, but it was just control,
The art of manipulation, mastered in silence

Jupiter's Game
Push & Pull

You whispered your truths in layers

I wore them like a veil

The world couldn't see the cracks, but

I felt them beneath my skin.

Your hands, once warm with care,

left scars hidden in the air… as I

danced in your illusion

unravelling threads I didn't know were

there

Under the Veil

I was the reflection of your
unspoken desires,
a mirror you shattered with a
careless touch,
Now I stand, fragmented yet whole,
the shards of your love scattered in

My Wake

You reflected yourself in my eyes,
made me believe I was the one broken.
But now, I see through the glass – it
was never me.
The fractures were yours to fix, the
lies were yours to untangle,
but I refused to stay a part of your
twisted game.
I walk away whole,
while you remain lost in the maze of
your own creation

The Mirrors of Manipulation

Gave you my love freely,
but you took it as a mere possession
and now,
I stand in the ruins of your
selfishness,
a monument to what you thought
you could claim

Baia

A ring, a gesture, a moment held high,

but in its shadow,

we watched it die.

What once was my storm, my bitter sun,

a future built, then undone.

Whispers of forever

… were nothing but tethered –

a dream that never came,

just flickers of a love,

burning in shame

Galileo Halo

I let you think you had the power, but
I was the one holding the knife
and with each cut I made, I freed myself,
leaving you bleeding in the shadows
of your own demise

Romantic Mercenary

Your lies are a weight,
but I wear them like a crown –
A broken empress,
I am your downfall

The Silence That Was Left

My heart adorned you
but I t was never enough to satisfy
your hunger
Now I wear my own crown,
carved from the bones of the love
You devoured

Ricochet Effect

How do I mourn what never truly existed?

I want to be angry,

but I'm too tired to feel anything at all.

And yet,

I ache for your touch.

How could I want something so broken?

emotional sadism

I once thought your touch was
healing, but now I know it was only a
poison,
Slow and insidious,
until I became numb,
and the numbness became my

Sanctuary

I want to hate you,

but I can't.

I wish I could forget you,

but I won't.

Torn between the finality of goodbye

& the ache of yearning for something

that will never return

limbo of what-ifs

You only saw what you wanted to possess,
but now I stand in full view,
A woman you will never understand,
a woman free of your gaze.

Discernment

I know you will… this isn't the end, just a pause in our story.

I'll answer you with grace, as if nothing ever happened.

This isn't over. I refuse to believe it.

you're going to text me soon

How did I become so numb to your absence?
Was it your touch that dulled me,
or the endless waiting for a love that
never truly was?
These days, I am left with the echo of a
voice that will never call again

02:18am

I wonder, on rare occasion
what thoughts plague your mind,
but I am no longer bound to seek the answers
you chose not to give.

Your presence in my thoughts has become a
mere formality

dismissed

I walked away, but still hear your voice in my head.

Is this the cost of love?

A constant replay of what was? The moments of tenderness dancing with the sting of betrayal?

I don't know how to silence it.

psychosis

There is a strange and unfamiliar relief,
in knowing I no longer need to chase
something that was slipping
through my fingers.
I can breathe now,
but I am still unsure if I want to.

Inner Conflict

Building a world of lies,
but I walked through the wreckage
you created
I've found the truth in the ruins.
I see now that I was –
I was never just the rose with thorns.
I was the garden you neglected,
the strength you never knew you'd
lose.
Now, the truth is mine to keep

Truths carved in Lies

Everyday, you slip further away
what once felt like fire now feels like ash.
I see the illusion for what it was –
a prison wrapped in affection… and
the chains are loosening
with each breath,
I breathe myself back to life

The Fading of a Misery

I walked through your hell, you watched me
burn
but what you didn't see
was that the flames did not consume me,
they only forged me into

Something New

Turning your destructive love into weapons,
slicing through your lies with surgical
precision
and now,
I wear your betrayal like a crown of thorns,
you'll feel it forever

the sting

But I broke you instead,
you'll carry the weight of my rage
for the rest of your days,
a scar you'll never escape

Gulag

While you tried to drown me in your indifference, I learned how to breathe underwater Now, I swim in the depths of your deceit, leaving you to gasp for air.

Plutonian Mermaid

Watching you drown in your own deceit
I learned to swim in the depths of your lies,
Now, I am the current that carries me away,
while you sink

tangled in your own web

Scattered

like glass at your feet

and now you're walking

barefoot,

cutting yourself on what you never

understood

Shattered

You whispered love,

but it was a soundless scream,

a cry for control,

and I was the puppet in your hands, but now

I am the one who holds the strings, and you

will

dance at my mercy

I was the storm you never saw coming, I tore
through your lies, and now I stand,
a tempest that left nothing but

Ruin

I wanted to scream,

to tear apart the echoes of your name, but

all I could do was breathe –

and I'm no longer sure

if the numbness is protection

or a sign of

how far I've fallen

If I just keep the silence,

If I make myself small enough –

Maybe you'll see me again.

Maybe if I hadn't sobbed so much, or if I hadn't loved you so deeply, things would've turned out differently.

I'll hold a little longer

If I wait long enough, maybe you'll realise how much you lost.

I'll hold my breath until you do.

I wake up to the same silence, it's suffocating
this emptiness that I carry with me.
How did I let you become my world?
I don't recognise myself anymore,
in this skin, in this heart
This broken thing that I've become.
How do I move on when I've given everything to
a shadow?
How do I heal

when the wound was self-inflicted?

Caught between freedom and longing, relief
and regret.
I should feel stronger than this.

seeds of doubt

A wordless finality.

A woman with an empty heart & a mind full of silence.

I should feel grief but instead,

I feel nothing.

Is this what it looks like?

Liberation

You were poison wrapped in velvet, a kiss that
burned with every word,
A touch that left scars I can't erase.
How dare you turn my love into a weapon I
didn't even know how to defend against?

I curse you for every lie, in every life
For the days spent in your shadow,
for the pieces of me I lost along the way.
You were not worth the weight I carried for us

Venom

My ego tells me to move on,
to burn your memory altogether
but my heart lingers in the past,
yearning for a contact that will never come.
Will I ever feel whole again, or will I always be incomplete?

the other half of Me

Stealing pieces of my fragile soul
with every cunning word you spoke,
and now – richer than you'll ever know,
you're left with nothing but

dust

I feed you a feast of –

a feast of my indifference,

eat it greedily,

but now, it suffocates you.

A poison you can't expel,

and I laugh

from the distance you created

I was never stitched together by you, I am
woven from shadows and fire,
Now, I burn your memory from the inside out

Seams

You used to hold me in your hands,
but now I am the blade you cut
yourself on,
sharper than your words,
colder than your touch, and I will
carve myself free
from the remnants of your love

Tattoo

I have turned the page, and you are but a fleeting chapter

A footnote in the book of my rage.

Last face

You loved the idea of me, never the
woman I am, and now I'm a ghost to you,
Unseen, uncaptured
vanishing into the silence left behind

That Sunday in September

I fed you my vulnerability,
& you never understood the power in it
Now I stand unshaken,
a fortress built from the ruins of your
manipulation

Power Play

You tried to pull me int your chaos,
but I was always the calm in the storm,
and now in the eye of your madness,
I watch it

consume You

Once I was your obsession,

but now – your waking nightmare,

A shadow that follows you everywhere you

go,

until you forget where you began,

and I became the only truth you can't

outrun

Once I thought you were my saviour,

but now, I know

You were the executioner,

and I, the victim,

not of fate,

but of your hands,

and I rise from your grave.

A Knight in Disguise

You loved me in pieces,
but those pieces were always broken,
I thought I could patch them
together, but now I see,
the fragments were meant to stay
scattered, like your love,

Unfixable & Void.

You thought you were the storm,
but I am the ocean,
endless and vast,
and your storm will pass,
while I remain, steady and unbroken.

Yemanjá

You thought you could erase me from your memory,
but I am a mark on your soul,
that will haunt you for as long as you breathe

the scar you can't hide

Oh, how I miss the chaos –
the drama, the tears, the endless longing.
How could I ever forget the joy of never
knowing where I stood?
The unpredictability of your love was truly
something special, wasn't it?
You loved the idea of me –
a convenient distraction, a plaything you
could use at will. How charming.
I'm sure you'll be just fine without me. After
all, you always were.
I was just a side note, a temporary fix. Nothing
more than a warm body to fill your inner void

It's almost poetic.

I don't miss you, I miss the idea of you –
the version I made up in my head,
The one who never existed,
but was always so easy to love.
Funny how we fall in love with our own fantasies.
I suppose I'll send you a "thank you" note
for the lesson in

self destruction

Feeling the weight of my own
disappointment, heavy
A constant reminder of how I failed – failed
to see you for what you were,
Failed to love myself enough to walk away
sooner

in retrospect

For what once seemed a great loss has now
revealed itself to be
nothing more than the clearing &
realigning of my path.
In my departure, I found freedom I
never knew I was owed.

mourning moment in the abyss

There's a strange satisfaction in knowing
that I was right, that I saw you for what
you were,
but there's also pain in the realisation
that I allowed myself to fall for you in
the first place

32nd

The weight of your memory no longer saddens or angers me.

It has faded, slipping into oblivion, where it belongs.

walking in the light of my own creation.

The residue of your name no longer stains

my lips,

nor does it echo in my thoughts.

You are but a relic of a time that no longer

holds relevance

how insignificant you have become

& to think I once measured my worth by the shadows you cast. How foolish.
For I have always been Ra
& your presence is nothing but a fading memory
of a time when I allowed myself to be blind

tainted

My light was once dimmed,
but you forgot, I'm the moon,
and in the darkness,
I shine brighter,
a reflection of everything you can never touch

Kynthos

I once thought you would ignite my soul,
but now I see you –
a mere flicker in the dark,
outshone by the stars I've learned to
trust

I was never lost, just blind.

and now, I see –

I've always had the power to

walk away.

You never owned me.

Not really.

The chains you forged in the name of love have
dissolved,
and I walk freely now,
untouched by your fetters, unperturbed by
your uncomfortable presence

forged

Now it all seems so trivial,
a whisper that has lost its power, I have
traded it for silence
& the peace it grants is far more precious
than the illusion you once sold me

the void left behind

I've learned to forgive myself, for the
time I wasted,
for the moments I spent hoping, for the
dream I once held.
Now, I live in reality & it is far more
satisfying than the illusion you ever
could provide

thoughts in Thessaloniki

You were a reflection of my own
brokenness,
I see it clearly now. I don't need
you anymore.
I don't even need the lies.

acceptance

I no longer wish for what we never had,

for what we could never be.

I have come to see that I was never the

problem –

you were the lesson

You are no longer a puzzle I wish to solve, for I am reacquainted with my own path, & it no longer makes logical sense to wind through the fog of your false promises

Touche

You were never my prince, my salvation, though I once thought you might be. I've found the peace I sought, not in your arms, but in the deep realms of my own strength, the wisdom that comes with

Rapunzel Awakening

I no longer search for answers, for there
are none you could offer
that would soothe the wounds you so
carelessly inflicted.
I have healed, not because of you

but in spite of you.

I do not wish you well, or harm.

You are merely a forgotten fragment of a

life that no longer concerns me

farewell Jupiter

Growing stronger in the soil you poisoned,

Now,

I am the flower you can never pick,

Rooted in the truth you can never grasp.

End note

Thank you Jupiter, for the fire you set
Within me.

For every omission, every twisted word
And every tear you never saw, you
Taught me one thing above all:
How to free myself from the mirage.

Thank you for the clarity in your chaos
And the strength in your absence.

May you live forever in the shadows you
Built for yourself.

Epilogue of the heart

In the quiet aftermath, I see the fragments for what they
Truly are – pieces of a life once consumed by shadows, now transformed into light.

Each poem, a step through wreckage, each word, a
Shard I've learned to hold without bleeding.

This collection isn't just a story of loss, but of
Reclamation. Of learning to breathe in the void and discovering the strength in solitude. It is an ode to those
Who dare to walk through the fire and emerge whole, even
When scarred.

To you, my beloved reader, may these words be a mirror, a
Sanctuary, or a storm – whatever you need them to be.

Fragments fade, but the lessons endure.

About the Author

Venusian Alchemist is a creative force whose words flow from the deep, emotional currents of her life, capturing the essence of transformation and self- realization.

With a profound understanding of the complexities of love, pain & rebirth, she crafts stories that resonate with those who seek to understand the beauty of their scars and the power within them.

Her journey has led her through toxic relationships and moments of deep self-

reflection, only to emerge with a greater understanding of herself and the strength to reclaim her narrative.

This poem book is a reflection of her healing process – an offering to those who may feel they are lost in the shadows of their own heartache. The purpose of this publication

is to connect with those who have walked similar paths, to remind them that even in the depths of despair, there is power to be found.

Each poem is a step toward freedom, a reclamation of the soul's voice, a declaration of rebirth.

Behind the pseudonym, Venusian Alchemist is a woman who embraces both the light and the dark, knowing that only through the darkest moments can the brightest truths be uncovered.

This poem book is an invitation to those who are ready to face their own shadows and emerge with a strength they never thought possible

Printed in Great Britain
by Amazon